Heaths and he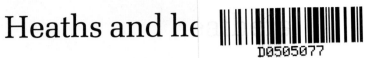

D0505077

Cover: the heather garden at Wisley in March, photograph by Michael Warren.
Overleaf: the heather garden at Wisley.

Heaths and heathers

A Wisley handbook

F. P. Knight

Cassell

The Royal Horticultural Society

Cassell Educational Limited
1 Vincent Square
London, SW1P 2PN
for the Royal Horticultural Society

First published 1972
New edition, fully revised and reset 1986

British Library Cataloguing in Publication Data

Knight, F. P.
  Heaths and heathers. — New ed. — (Wisley
  handbook)
  1. Heathers
  I. Title II. Series
  635.9′3362   SB413.H42

  ISBN 0-304-31091-3

Photographs by Michael Warren and F. P. Knight
Phototypesetting by Franklyn Graphics, Formby
Printed in Hong Kong by Wing King Tong Co. Ltd

Contents

	page
Heathers in nature	8
Heathers in the garden	10
Choice of site	10
Preparation of the soil	10
Design and layout	12
Planting	18
When to plant	18
How to plant	18
Aftercare	21
Pruning	21
Mulching	23
Propagation	24
Layering	24
Cuttings	26
Seeds	28
Problems	30
Pests	30
Diseases	30
Choosing heathers	32
Species	32
Hybrids	36
Cultivars	38
Shrubs to use in the heather garden	57
Conifers	60
Books	64

The common names, heaths and heathers, are used for three main genera – *Calluna, Daboecia* and *Erica*. There are few plants which have so deservedly gained recognition for their wide and effective use in modern gardening. The variations in size, habit of growth, colour of flower and foliage, and flowering times, together with the satisfactory way in which heathers blend with other plants in the garden, result in one of the most satisfying of garden features. As evergreens they contribute interest throughout the year. It is true that their use is restricted to suitable soil types, for with few exceptions heathers will not tolerate alkaline soils. Heaths and heathers are of particular use in cutting down work in the garden. When planted in groups each grows into its neighbour, so leaving little opportunity for weeds to grow.

A visit to any nursery or garden centre selling hardy trees and shrubs will show the wide range of heathers available. Today, many are grown in containers, so that planting can be carried out at almost any time of the year.

No garden is too large or too small for heathers to be fitted in, either as a complete heather garden, or in groups among shrubs, to cover sloping banks, or in the rock garden.

I strongly advise anyone who is planning to plant heathers to see as many existing heather gardens as possible. There are good examples at the Royal Horticultural Society's Garden at Wisley, the Savill Garden at Windsor, the Royal Botanic Gardens in Edinburgh and at Kew, the Liverpool University Botanic Garden, Ness, in Cheshire, and the Northern Horticultural Society's garden at Harlow Car, near Harrogate.

Although these are examples on a large scale, they clearly show effective planning and planting which can be adapted for any size of garden by adjusting the numbers of plants required and, if planning for a small garden, omitting those, such as the tree heaths, which will grow too large.

A corner of a heather garden.

Heathers in nature

More species of *Erica* are to be found wild in southern Africa than in any other country, although these Cape heaths are not hardy here and so will not be considered further. The heathers which cover large tracts of moorland and mountain in Britain and the rest of Europe belong to the genera *Calluna, Daboecia* and *Erica*. These are the hardy heathers that we can grow outside.

Calluna vulgaris is the purple heather, or ling, of the mountains and moors, and the observant will notice a considerable variation in the habit of growth of the plants and also in colours of flowers and foliage. Plants may be small close-growing hummocks or shrubs up to 3 feet high (90cm).

Erica is the botanical name for heaths, but it is usual to include both *Calluna* and *Erica* in the term 'heather' – for instance the *heather* garden. The hardy species of *Erica* are natives of Europe, and eight are found in the British Isles. All are evergreen shrubs, with very small linear leaves. The flowers are produced in abundance at the ends of the shoots, and do not drop when they fade, remaining on the stems and turning to an attractive russet brown colour.

Daboecia, the third member of the heaths and heathers, includes two species but only one is usually seen in gardens. *Daboecia cantabrica*, St Dabeoc's heath, is a native of Ireland, where it is often found threading itself through the autumn-flowering gorse.

The conditions in which these plants grow in Europe are broadly similar. The ericas and *Calluna* cover large areas of higher land where the soil is usually rather poor and the rainfall sometimes high. Some grow in damp places, others where the soil dries out in summer. These are usually exposed parts of the country with little protection from cold and strong winds.

It is worth mentioning some of the individual needs among ericas. For instance, *Erica ciliaris*, Dorset heath, although growing in moist soils in nature (not swamps), will tolerate drier conditions in cultivation, especially when peat has been added to the soil. *Erica cinerea* always grows in drier places than *Calluna*. *Erica tetralix*, cross-leaved heath, grows wild in wetter conditions than most other species and thrives in wet bogs where cotton grass may be a companion plant. Although native of Cornwall and Ireland, *Erica vagans* (Cornish heath) grows well in culti-

'Gold Tips', a cultivar of the tree heath *Erica arborea*.

vation as far north as the Moray Firth; it will tolerate slightly alkaline soil conditions. *Erica herbacea* (*carnea*)* and its numerous cultivars will also tolerate alkaline soils. At Wisley this heather grew successfully on a steep, north facing bank. Two taller heathers are *Erica arborea* (tree heath) and *E. lusitanica* (Portuguese heath); both are liable to be damaged in severe winters, but both are tolerant of slightly alkaline soil conditions.

The environment in which heathers grow wild tends to be harsh, with poor soil and little shelter. They are brought up to a tough life, but given a little care in the garden will repay the gardener for many seasons. The only condition is that heathers must be planted in full sun.

*The correct specific name *herbacea* is used in this book, although the plant is still listed as *Erica carnea* in nursery catalogues.

Heathers in the garden

The question of planting to reduce maintenance crops up many times in the life of a professional nurseryman. Heather gardening contributes largely to saving labour and particularly by cutting down weeding.

The use of heathers in the garden can vary from planting small groups along the foot of shrub borders or beds, the formation of a formal edging along the side of a path (but this does not appeal to me), in beds consisting entirely of heathers with a few carefully selected and sited dwarf or slow-growing conifers and other suitable shrubs (for suggestions see pp. 57–63), in the rock garden, and best of all, where there is room, in a separate heather garden. In short there is every reason, given suitable soil conditions, for all gardens to have their quota of heathers, for these will provide colour throughout the year.

CHOICE OF SITE

From my experience of gardening in several parts of the United Kingdom, on soils varying in texture and with annual rainfall amounts from 20 to 45 inches (500–1200 mm), I can say that heathers will thrive in a wide range of conditions. They like to be in the sunshine since if planted in shade they become straggly and soft in growth and fail to flower freely. It will have been noticed, however, that an exception cited earlier was *Erica herbacea*, growing on a northern slope at Wisley; I want to emphasise that there is a difference between growing in an open exposed northern slope and under the shade of trees, and the latter is not a suitable situation for heathers.

Many sloping grass banks which are difficult to maintain can be planted with heathers and rocks installed to provide an additional attractive feature. Such an arrangement associated with the right shrubs could transform an area that was a troublesome chore into one of low maintenance.

PREPARATION OF THE SOIL

Preparation for planting heathers normally consists of single digging, breaking up the soil and removing all weeds. Perennial weeds, in particular all pieces of bindweed and couch grass, must

A mixture of *Erica herbacea* in Windsor Great Park.

be removed; they are very difficult to control after planting. Single digging means digging to a depth of one spade. Peat should be worked into the soil (but be sure the peat is damp); I prefer to do this by spreading a layer up to 2 inches deep (5 cm) over the surface of the ground after digging and working this in around the roots when planting, taking care to mix it in with the soil.

In a heavy clayey soil drainage can be improved by throwing up the soil when digging so that the level of the bed is a few inches above that of the surrounding soil. This raised area will dry out more quickly as the water drains down to the lower level. Adding a generous supply of peat will also help to improve a heavy soil.

On lighter and stony soils heathers will grow satisfactorily, and there is no need to make the raised beds as the drainage on these types of soils is likely to be very good. In a hot dry period the drainage will probably be too sharp, but the water-holding capacity of the soil can be improved by mixing in peat, with more peat being added and mixed in each spring.

The important point to be emphasised is that thorough preparation of the soil before planting will result in vigorous, healthy growth of the plants.

11

DESIGN AND LAYOUT

The design of a heather garden is a matter of scale and balance, demanding the adaption of the available site, summing up its setting and size, and then designing and carrying out a planting scheme which fits. In the large heather garden at the west end of Seven Acres in Wisley Garden less than about fifty plants of one kind would be inadequate. In an average sized garden groups of twenty-five, fifteen or even fewer plants would look right.

The ideal, of course, is to be able to plant the whole heather garden in one co-ordinated operation. Where this is possible I like to have the area prepared in the manner I have described and then, to invest the scheme with character, the soil on a flat or even surface can be skilfully undulated so that the planting looks natural. This can be done by building up gently rounded mounds of soil, not sharp peaks, between which will be valleys, and these mounds and valleys will be accentuated by planting drifts of taller growing plants on the mounds and lower spreading kinds in the valleys. There is so much one can accomplish on a flat site by adopting some of the effects to be seen in the wild.

Heathers in Adrian Bloom's garden at
Bressingham, Norfolk, provide year-round interest.

Having prepared the site and given it some character the next operation is to plan the planting. This can be done in two main ways, the first being that of taking a fairly accurate survey of the site to be planted and plotting this on a drawing board to a workable scale, for example that of an inch (2.5 cm) to 8 feet (2.4 m). Assuming that the choice of heathers has already been made, the next question is how many of each are required and how to arrange them. For this, information is needed on the colours of the flowers and foliage, times of flowering and particularly the eventual size of the plants. In addition allowance must be made for including others plants, such as *Pernettya mucronata* and conifers, which associate well with heathers.

The sizes of the individual groups will depend mainly on the size of the site. This also influences the provision of suitable paths. On a large scale grass paths may be appropriate; in small schemes paths through the heathers may not be needed and flat stepping-stones or just the beaten earth will suffice. There is always the danger of being 'too tidy' and I do not like to see a neatly edged lawn meeting the natural growth of the plants; I like to see irregular paths following the natural run of the ground.

It is now that scale and balance take over. In designing the irregular shapes of the planting areas which each group will occupy, I have derived much help by thinking of a coloured map of England where the counties in their different shapes and sizes are portrayed by different colours. These make ideal pictures in the mind of groups of heathers which can be adapted and transferred to a drawing. Next comes the work of filling in the names and quantities of the plants to be used.

In all planting schemes worked out on a drawing board I find it practical to make a careful list of the plants I wish to use. I divide my list under the three main headings, tall, intermediate and low growing kinds, and then fill in details on dimensions, colour of flower and foliage, and time of flowering. I call this my master list and treat it as if it were a reservoir of plant material into which I dip as the planning progresses, transferring the names of the particular plants to the positions I decide as appropriate on the plan. Small points, such as doing the original work on the drawing with a soft pencil, should be kept in mind, for seldom will the first scheme be the last one.

Spacing of the individual plants to be used within each localised group is of primary importance. I know that there is some disagreement, and in the following I give my basic distances and leave it to others either to adopt or adapt them. I like to establish a complete cover over the ground as quickly as possible, and therefore space the smaller growing cultivars of *Erica herbacea*, such

as 'King George', at one foot apart (30 cm). The larger growing cultivars of E. herbacea, such as 'Springwood White' need more room, 15 inches or more (37 cm) (see list on pp. 39 for measurements). Calluna vulgaris and its tall cultivars such as 'Alportii' I space at 15 inches (37 cm), Erica erigena (mediterranea) at 2 feet 6 inches (75 cm) and tree heathers at 4 feet (1.2 m). Some people may think that my spacing of the smaller growing kinds is too close, but these are the distances I have found practical after planting thousands of heathers. Within the pattern I have set out there are many heathers and heaths of intermediate growth and spacing can therefore be adjusted. For myself, if ever I find I am caught hesitating between spreading out or closing up the spacing I close up. The sooner the ground is covered and the weeds excluded the better. With planting at wider distances than those I have given above, the plant canopy over the soil takes longer to meet and to suppress the weeds. Plants that are relatively widely spaced do, however, become a better, individual shape, because they are not competing with their neighbours; but this is not my way of growing heathers.

The most practical method for transferring a paper plan to the soil is to mark out the planting scheme on the ground. With this method the pencil used for drawing gives place to canes and labels. We are back at the stage where the ground has been dug and gentle mounds and little valleys have been made. The soil surface will need to be reasonably fine so that marking out is not made too difficult through encountering too many obstructions. The same mind picture of the final scheme must dominate as when designing on the drawing board, so cull information from the reservoir of plant material to be used and the shapes of the English counties on the map.

Sum up the whole site so that the irregularly shaped groups can be marked out on the ground in an appropriate and balanced way. Then take a stick or tool handle and mark out the boundaries of the various groups on the surface of the soil by a depression sufficiently deep to be readily seen; this can easily be filled in if the first shapes are not right. As a precaution, and particularly if there is a chance of the marks being obliterated by rain before planting, then some sand or sawdust can be strewn along the channels to show where they are.

I have found that I make a better job if the major marking out of the planting scheme can be completed in one operation, simply because I find I am not always in the mood to pick up where I left off.

Above, 'King George', a small growing cultivar of Erica herbacea. Below, the larger 'Springwood White' (see pp. 41 and 42).

Spacing when planting heathers (see pp. 13–15).

Having finally decided that the scheme marked out is a good one, the next step is to fill in the groups. Whereas on the drawing board the names of the plants to be used will be written in the appropriate spaces on the planting plan, in the open-ground scheme labels are placed on the individual marked out groups, either labels which are stuck in the ground or paper labels tied to canes. In both cases a control list with the names of the plants to be used must be prepared beforehand and the names and quantities written on the labels. Knowledge of the plants to be used and imagination to visualise the end result are both essential in placing the right labels in the right positions. Based on my own experience it will, I think, be found that one acquires a flair for what is required, a rather slow hesitant uncertainty at the beginning seems suddenly to give way to a creative urge to get on and 'make a good job of it'. One begins to enjoy the exercise and when the final adjustment of the labels has been made there comes a feeling of deep satisfaction. Here I repeat the advice given earlier to visit and study existing established heather gardens, and adapt what is seen, to ensure that the planting is pleasing to one's self.

The heather garden at the Northern Horticultural Society's Garden, Harlow Car, Yorkshire.

17

Planting

WHEN TO PLANT

Now that container-grown plants are widely available, the time when it is possible to plant many shrubs, including heaths and heathers, has been greatly extended. Great emphasis used to be placed on planting heathers in the autumn and the spring, but in those days the plants were largely raised in the open ground. While the best times to plant are still between early October and early December, and late February to mid-April, it is now possible to plant in winter provided that the soil is not frozen, and in summer provided that the plants are kept well watered. Another advantage of buying container-grown plants (and in addition to garden centres, most specialist suppliers of heathers will also be able to provide plants in pots) is that there is less urgency to plant immediately, and the work can be conveniently spread over as long a period as one wishes.

HOW TO PLANT

After the preparation of the soil has been carried out, and the plants obtained, the actual planting is carried out. The planting distances given on p. 15 need not be adhered to rigidly, but it is generally more satisfactory if the plants do not overlap from one group to the next.

Having made sure that the complete balls of soil in which the plants have been growing are thoroughly saturated, remove them from their containers. It will usually be found that the plants are so well established in their containers that there is a 'cocoon' of roots enclosing the balls of soil. This should be loosened and separated out by prodding with the tines of a hand fork, or a strong sharply pointed stick. Never plant with the roots in a close matted state, as this results in the plants just sitting in the ground for too long a time before new roots are pushed out into the surrounding soil.

Another problem is what to do with the roots which have grown through the drainage holes of clay or plastic pots. There may sometimes be more roots outside than inside the pots, particularly when they have been standing on a bed of peat or similar material. The temptation is to wrench off the protruding roots, but this

Above, removing the plant from its polythene bag and, below, firming in the plant.

upsets the balance between top growth and the root system, so that the tip shoots start to die back. Plants in plastic pots, which usually have several drainage holes, are sometimes difficult to deal with, and I usually cut these downwards from the rim with an old pair of secateurs to release the root system. Plants grown in polythene film containers are easily removed. I always remove

19

any drainage crocks which may have been placed in the bottoms of the pots, but the old practice of crocking when growing heathers is not so often met with now.

The heathers having been set out they now have to be planted. A trowel is the best tool for this. It is more practical to start planting at the point farthest away from a path or lawn and work towards the point of completion. A skilled gardener works with rhythm, making up the surface of the ground as he proceeds, leaving the minimum of tidying up to be done at the finish.

The depth of planting should be such that the point where the base of the stems of the heathers emerges from the soil in the container is buried about an inch (2.5 cm) below the surface of the ground. This allows for settling and the top of the ball of soil will finally come just below the surface. Planting should be firm and the peat on the surface worked in around the roots of the plants. Avoid planting too deeply as this results in new fine roots being developed on the buried portion of the stems with a corresponding lack of new root action from the old root system; in times of drought the delicate roots produced on the stems will suffer.

So much for container-grown plants, but what of those which have been dug up from the open ground? With these the objective is to prevent the exposed roots from drying out between the time of lifting and replanting. Too many plants should not be laid out at one time. It is better to leave most where they keep moist and only unpack convenient quantities as they can be planted. It is obvious that one does not have the same freedom of handling as with container-grown plants, for each time a plant has to be moved it will mean that some of the fine soil adhering to its roots must be shaken off. Although more care has to be taken when planting open-ground plants they have one advantage over the container-grown specimens in that their root systems do not need to be dealt with so drastically.

So far I have been describing the work required in planting a new heather garden, but there are no fundamental differences in dealing with more modest schemes. If only part of a shrub border or some heather beds are involved, the advice already given can be adapted. The ground preparation will be the same and there will be no difference in handling the plants. Appropriate schemes can be attained by planting small groups of different kinds to give a more striking display over a shorter time. The same applies to planting heathers in a rock garden or on a sloping bank.

Aftercare

Heathers will need some attention after planting and it will be found that this settles down in normal conditions to a repetitive programme. After autumn and winter planting the plants will need to be firmed following a period of frost, and the staking and tying of the tree heaths should be checked. Snow lodging in the taller growing plants can be carefully shaken off to prevent or reduce branches breaking under its weight. Spring and summer planting may be followed by a drought and a good soaking should be given when needed; it is best to apply the water in the evenings, so that the plants can absorb the moisture in the lower temperatures overnight.

Weeding will be required during the first year or two but will get less as the plants grow together and cover the bare ground. I use both a hoe and my hands, and take care that I do not hoe too deeply and disturb the surface roots. When hand weeding I also use a hand fork to deal with any deep rooting perennial weeds.

At the present time there are a limited number of proprietary weedkillers containing simazine available to the amateur; these are suggested for use in rose beds but can be used among trees and shrubs. It is recommended that those who wish to use one among heathers should first carry out a trial on their own particular soil conditions and then proceed in accordance with the results obtained. Strict attention should be paid to the instructions so clearly given by the manufacturers on the rate and method of application.

PRUNING

Some moderate cutting back does give good results in shaping the plants and maintaining their vigour.

For pruning, heaths and heathers can be divided into three groups: 1. summer flowering; 2. winter flowering; 3. tree heaths, such as Erica australis, E. erigena (mediterranea) and E. terminalis.

The summer flowering kinds should be very lightly pruned in the first half of March every year by cutting back, with a pair of sharp garden shears, the old flower heads to a point just below the bottom flowers on the stems. Do not cut back in the old wood. This pruning is followed by the production of vigorous shoots which will provide flowers of a high quality in the summer. If

21

A heather garden in winter.

plants are left unpruned the new growths tend to be stubby and the flower spikes shorter.

The winter flowering kinds are cut back in the same way immediately after flowering to a point below the bottom flowers. This is normally done in late March and early April.

It will be found in practice that with heathers and heaths which tend to be procumbent in growth more skill is required in getting at the points where pruning should be done. But the care spent on the plants will be amply repaid, by better growth and flowering.

The third group does not need annual pruning. If the plants need to be rejuvenated, or reduced in size, cutting back can be done in late April or early May. It is difficult to prescribe a general operation, and generally it is best to take each plant or group of plants on its merits. Straggling branches can be shortened with secateurs, and the tall leading branches of *Erica arborea* which are outstripping all the others and making the bushes look 'thin' can be cut back to restore more balanced growth. If rejuvenation

22

Erica cinerea 'Eden Valley', which flowers from early June (see p. 49).

is needed, but the bushes are fairly healthy (i.e. their leaves are green) then fairly drastic cutting back can be carried out. Even if severely damaged by frost and snow most plants will respond well to hard pruning. New shoots are usually produced and by the second season most of them will be growing vigorously again.

In the wild, heather is often burnt every few years to provide new young shoots for the sheep, but this method of promoting fresh growth is not for the garden.

MULCHING

I like to give my plants an annual mulch with peat in spring after the pruning has been done. The peat is worked in between the plants to form a layer on the surface about half an inch deep (1.5 cm). Pulverised bark is an alternative mulching material.

23

Propagation

Nearly all the heaths and heathers which we grow in our garden are cultivars and must therefore be propagated vegetatively because they do not come true from seed. Two types of vegetative propagation that are commonly used to propagate heathers are described below.

LAYERING

For the amateur who wishes to raise small stocks of heathers in his garden and has no specialised equipment for propagation by cuttings, layering is the method which requires a minimum of skill or equipment. Layering means treating the stems of the plant before removing it from the plant so that new roots are produced; the rooted portions are then removed and planted to form new plants.

There are various ways of doing this. If the parent plant is to be retained without spoiling or moving it, a few branches around the perimeter can be selected and pegged to the ground so that a few inches of the stems are buried. It is usual to loosen the surface of the soil and mix in a little sand and peat to form a small local propagation bed. Then the selected stems are firmly fixed into this, using wooden pegs or bent wires, or even by placing stones on the branches. I find the use of stones somewhat clumsy and prefer pegs. It is not necessary to cut or scrape the stems before burying them. Layering is very successful if done in late September and October. After about a year sufficient roots are established to enable the new plants to be cut from the parent plant and then preferably planted in a nursery-bed for about six months before putting them in their permanent positions.

Another simple method of layering is to part the branches of the growing plant at the soil surface and sprinkle in between a mixture of sand and peat. This should be pressed down as firmly as possible, so that the branches root into it. Topping up can be done as the material gets washed in by the winter rains. This method of layering can also be done in the autumn.

Above, layering by (left) making a trench round the plant, then (right) spreading out the branches and filling in the centre.
Below, *Erica tetralix* 'Pink Star' flowers from June to October (see p. 50).

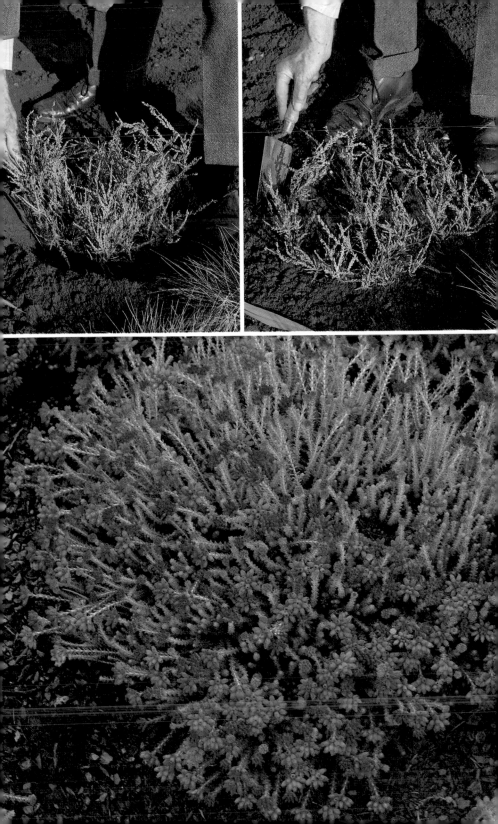

The object in both the methods described should be to get vigorous young plants and not to try to root long straggling branches. In the second method the mound should rise so that the rooting takes place as near as possible to the active green leafy portions, in order to provide shapely plants. Sometimes in order to get larger plants more quickly several of the newly rooted young stems are bunched together and planted as one unit.

CUTTINGS

More heathers are raised from cuttings than by any other method and today there are several successful ways in which this can be done. One is to insert them in pots or pans and place these in a warm frame or greenhouse. The current method used at Wisley is as follows:

Cuttings, $2\frac{1}{2}$ inches long (6 cm), are taken in July, either of tip growths or side growths pulled off from the branches with a heel, that is with a very small portion of the branch adhering to the base of the cutting. If the heel should be long and ragged it is trimmed off with a sharp knife or razor blade; no leaves are removed from the cuttings. They are inserted about $\frac{1}{2}$ inch (1.5 cm) deep in a mixture of 2 parts sand and 1 part sphagnum moss peat in 5- or 6-inch diameter pans (15 cm), in which a piece of broken pot has been placed to prevent the mixture filtering through the drainage hole. Normally a 5-inch pan will take 50 to 60 cuttings. The pans are placed on a bed of sand on an open staging with a bottom heat of 70°F (21°C) in a warm greenhouse under an intermittent mist spray controlled by an electronic leaf or balance switch.

The cuttings produce sufficient roots in three to six weeks, depending on the species or cultivar, and are then potted singly into $2\frac{1}{2}$-inch pots (6 cm), or pricked off at the rate of 30 rooted cuttings into $2\frac{1}{2}$-inch deep seed trays (6 cm). The compost used is two parts acid loam, two parts moss peat and one part sand.

The trays or pots are then put into cold frames, which are kept closed at first. Then as the new young plants become established, air is admitted until finally the frame lights are removed, at first for limited periods in suitable weather but replaced during bad weather in the winter. In the first spring after the initial insertion of the cuttings, the young plants are ready for planting out in the open straight into their permanent position or into a nursery bed until the following autumn.

The amateur gardener without mist or a cold frame can still easily propagate from cuttings. The cuttings are taken in July, but the shoots selected are shorter than those for rooting under mist, and are about 1 to $1\frac{1}{4}$ inches long (2.5–3 cm). The cuttings are not trimmed and are inserted in the same mixture as above, either in pots which are then put in a closed cold frame, or direct in the cold frame. The former is preferred because then each cultivar can be kept separate; they can then be hardened off as they become rooted. This is important because there is a variation in the speed of rooting between many heather species and cultivars.

If you do not have a cold frame the pots can be put outside in the garden in a shady place, e.g. at the foot of a north-facing wall. The microclimate around the cuttings can be kept uniform in temperature and humidity by enclosing the pots in closed plastic bags, or preferably by using clear plastic domes. These are more satisfactory than plastic bags because they do not sag over the cuttings.

When I was at Kew we used bell-glasses and there is no doubt their use is comparatively trouble-free. It is not easy to obtain bell-glasses today although plastic 'bell-jars' are available. There are also ready-made propagators consisting of a plastic tray with a clear plastic cover in which is some means of ventilation. With one of these the amateur can root heather cuttings without the help of special propagating frames or other equipment. The bell-glass should be sited in the open garden in a position not exposed to the sun otherwise the temperature will fluctuate too widely between day and night. The small area of propagating bed required can be clearly defined by pressing the rim of the bell-glass (or other container) firmly on the surface of the soil. Within this shape excavate the soil with a hand fork to a depth of 3 inches (7.5 cm) and replace it with a mixture of 3 parts of fine peat and 1 part of sharp lime-free sand. Make this firm so that the finished surface is about half an inch (1.5 cm) above the soil surrounding the bell-glass. Give a good watering, with a fine rose on the can, about twenty-four hours before inserting the cuttings.

I prefer to take cuttings in early October. Short flowerless side-shoots of the current year's growth are taken from the parent branches about an inch long (2.5 cm). Although not strictly necessary, I still like to pull away the tiny shoots from the side of the older branches, and with a very sharp knife or razor-blade trim the minute heel at the base of the cutting. There is no need to remove the leaves. The cuttings are then inserted in the bed of peat and sand to about half of their length by using a fine dibber to make the individual holes. The cuttings must be firmly inserted, spaced about half an inch apart (1.5 cm). The cuttings should be watered-in and I like to finish off by sprinkling some very dry silver sand to fill in the irregularities on the surface. This is like sifting sugar on a cake. The circular area having been satisfactorily filled, the bell-glass is placed firmly over the cuttings, taking care that there is no space between the rim of the glass and the soil.

If the cuttings have been taken in October no attention is needed during the winter, except to keep a watchful eye on the fine soil surface in case this may be disrupted by worm casts; I have even had my work upset by a mole. The debris from worm casts should be removed and the surface firmed.

A little more attention will be needed from early March onwards. It is not unusual at that time to get warm days and this is when rooting will be accelerated. If there is a tendency for the soil around the bell-glass to dry out, water round without removing it. As the spring develops, and according to the weather, a little air can be admitted gradually by placing a wedge under the rim of the glass. To begin with this can be done for no more than two or three hours in the middle of the day, but the period of ventilation can be gradually increased until the whole glass can be removed for a time. By the end of June it can be left off altogether. It is impossible to set down a precise calendar of operations, so much depends on the weather.

In August or September the tiny rooted cuttings can be carefully pricked off into boxes or planted in a specially prepared nursery bed. The young plants are left there for about one year to grow on into a suitable size for transplanting to their permanent site.

SEEDS

Some plants can be raised from seeds and one often sees self-sown seedlings growing near the parent plants. For example, Erica terminalis has regenerated naturally in the chalky soil in the garden at Highdown, near Worthing in Sussex. I also remember establishing broad paths of Calluna vulgaris in a large woodland-moorland garden bordering Chobham Common. This was done by gathering branches of the Calluna from the wild when the seeds were ripe and shaking these over the path areas so that the seeds were scattered on the prepared surface of the ground. The result was very good. In another garden at Windlesham Moor heather paths which were established by this method were kept short and springy by regularly cutting the plants with an old lawnmower.

Above, Calluna vulgaris 'Annemarie', with double flowers produced in summer (see p. 42).
Below, the pink flowers of Calluna vulgaris 'Darkness' (see p. 43) contrasting with the bright green foliage of Erica lusitanica 'George Hunt' (see p. 42).

Problems

Heaths and heathers in gardens are little affected by pests. Rabbits are sometimes a nuisance when they graze down young plants and they are, of course, likely to be abundant on light sandy soils. Various proprietary chemical repellants are partially effective in preventing damage but such protection as they afford is likely to break down in the winter when alternative food supplies are limited. In these circumstances only physical barriers, such as small-mesh wire netting, will give young plants complete protection. Once plants are established they can usually tolerate a certain amount of grazing without permanent harmful effect.

Other pests, such as the heather beetle and the heather gall midge are only of minor importance in gardens, although the heather beetle may do temporary damage to ling growing wild on moorlands.

DISEASES

Very few diseases of heathers have been recorded in Britain. Those occurring most frequently are as follows:

Erica wilt or browning (*Phytophthora cinnamomi*). This disease has, in recent years, become very troublesome on certain cultivars of *Calluna vulgaris*, *Erica herbacea*, *E. cinerea*, *E. erigena* (*mediterranea*), *E. vagans* and *Erica* × *darleyensis*. The first obvious symptom is a silvering of the leaves on one or two shoots, the tips of which wilt. Within a few weeks some or all of the shoots die back, the affected plant loses many of its leaves and those which remain turn brown: occasionally, however, all the leaves become either grey or brown but are retained by the plant.

The fungus which causes this disease can attack a wide range of plants including conifers and rhododendrons. It is soil-borne and is encouraged by wet soil conditions. Infection occurs through the roots and most takes place during the summer when the soil is warm. The fungus produces thick-walled resting spores which can probably survive in the soil for several years and these can only be killed by steam sterilisation of the soil or by the use of soil sterilants which are not available to amateur gardeners. The disease is, therefore, difficult to control in small gardens and the best method is to dig up and burn any plants suspected of having the disease. Heathers should not be replanted where this disease has occurred unless the soil is first changed.

Unfortunately this disease can be positively identified only by specialised laboratory techniques and even then the results are not necessarily conclusive. Similar symptoms can, of course, be induced by adverse soil conditions and cultivated heathers can be affected in soils that are too dry, as well as too wet, even though they grow naturally in light soils which are inclined to dry out quickly. Should there be any doubt as to whether the discoloration of heather plants is due to faulty root action or erica wilt, it is recommended that, after removal of dead and dying shoots, the plants be sprayed fairly frequently during the growing season with a foliar feed. Nutrients applied in this form are taken in fairly rapidly by the leaves and the plants should receive a quick boost in vigour which will, in turn, encourage the development of new roots to replace those which have been injured or killed by the adverse soil conditions. If the plants do not recover after this treatment, they should be burned and the soil changed.

Honey fungus (*Armillaria* species). This fungus, is the most dangerous of all soil-borne parasites and can attack almost any type of plant. It has been known to kill plants of *Andromeda*, *Calluna* and *Erica*. The fungus kills the plant outright, and can be seen as fan-shaped masses of white fungal growth beneath the bark around the collar of the dead plant. Sometimes the brownish root-like structures (rhizomorphs), by which the fungus spreads through the soil, can be seen attached to the larger dead roots.

Affected plants should be dug up and burnt and the soil be changed completely. If possible, the source of infection (which may be an old stump or dead plant in a privet hedge for instance) should be traced and removed. If the trouble persists expert advice should be sought.

Rhizomorph fungus (*Marasmius androsaceus*). This fungus may kill plants of *Calluna* in Scotland, particularly in wet areas. It produces brown toadstools which soon turn black; these are very small, being about $1\frac{1}{4}$ inches high (3cm) with a cap of $\frac{1}{4}$ inch (5mm) and are not, therefore, easily seen. The toadstools are formed from July to November and produce numerous spores which give rise to more fungus plants, each of which produces fine black thread-like structures (rhizomorphs) which can be found at any time of the year wound round the heather stems. The rhizomorphs enter the stems and kill them so that the whole plant dies out. Affected plants should be removed and burned as there is no way of controlling the disease.

31

Choosing heathers

The choice of heather material is bewildering at first. Although there are relatively few species, there are hundreds of cultivars varying in flower colour, time of flowering and leaf colour. I will give first some details of the species and hybrids followed by a selection from the cultivars.

SPECIES

Calluna

Calluna vulgaris (heather, ling) grows up to 3 feet (90 cm), making a straggly, evergreen bush. The flowers are usually purplish pink but there are many variations in colour. The main flowering period is from July to November.

Daboecia

The species usually found in British gardens is *D. cantabrica*, a native of western Europe. It grows to 2 feet (60 cm), and the broad leaves are dark green above and whitish below. The flowers are rosy purple, oval, borne at the ends of the shoots from June to October.

Erica

The range of variation in ericas is very wide, and covers not only flower and leaf colour, but height, and among the species listed below tree heaths are included as well as the low growing kinds.

Erica arborea, tree heath, grows wild in a wide area around the Mediterranean, even down to the equator in Africa. It is not usually fully hardy here. It will grow up to to 20 feet (6 m), but is usually less than half this in cultivation in Britain. The leaves are bright green. Flowers are produced from February to April, and are nearly pure white, although sometimes with a pinkish tinge. Plants are always supplied in pots as they do not transplant well from the open ground. They need to be staked and tied after planting. The bushy habit should be encouraged by cutting back

Above, the tall Spanish heath *Erica australis* bears abundant bloom in midsummer (see p. 34).
Below, the Mediterranean *Erica erigena*, a small to medium shrub (see p. 34).

leading shoots that are too vigorous. It will tolerate mildly alkaline soils.

Erica australis, the Spanish heath, grows to about 4 feet (1.2m). It tends to spread out and does not always regain its original form after snow has lodged in the branches. The fragrant, bright purplish red flowers are produced in profusion in May and June, making an important link in the continuity of flowering. One of the most effective groupings of it that I have seen is with the Warminster broom (*Cytisus* × *praecox*). There is also a white flowered cultivar, 'Mr Robert', that was collected in southern Spain.

Erica ciliaris, the Dorset heath, is a native of south-west Europe, and of Dorset, Cornwall and west Ireland. It forms a low-growing shrub, up to 12 inches high (30 cm), with ascending shoots. The flowers are usually bright pink, and larger than most other ericas, being produced from July to October.

Erica cinerea, bell heather, is widely distributed in western Europe including the British Isles, forming a stiff branching shrub up to 24 inches tall (60 cm). When propagating I have noticed that as it grows on from rooted cutting to maturity it does not produce such a mass of very fine roots as do other species; plants tend to become surface rooting with fewer, larger main roots. The flowers are typically rosy purple, borne from June to September. It is particularly effective when seen with the dwarf gorses, *Ulex minor* or *U. galli*.

Erica erigena (*E. mediterranea*) comes from south western France, Spain and Portugal, and also western Ireland. It forms a vigorous, upright shrub of 3 to 12 feet tall (90 cm–3.6 m), producing purplish pink flowers from March to May. It is lime-tolerant and useful to provide height particularly in small gardens where *E. arborea* is too tall. The wood is brittle and branches are liable to snap if weighed down by snow, so knock it off as early as possible.

Erica herbacea, one of the best known of the heaths, is native of the mountains of central and southern Europe. It tolerates alkaline soil and is very hardy. Plants grow up to 6 inches tall (15 cm), being spreading in habit. The flowers are usually rosy red although there is a wide range of colour among the cultivars. It flowers during the period October to April, so no other heather contributes so much cheerfulness to the winter garden.

Erica lusitanica (Portuguese heath) is native of south west Europe and naturalised in south west England. It is a lovely plant even when not in flower, growing up to 8 feet (2.4 m) with feathery branches of pale green leaves. The tubular flowers are pinkish in bud opening to white; the main flowering period is March to May. Although not reliably hardy, E. *lusitanica* will tolerate mildly alkaline soils.

Erica *mackaiana* is a native of Co. Galway and Donegal, and also north west Spain. An attractive plant, it grows to about 9 inches (22 cm) high and bears rose coloured flowers in between July and September.

Erica *scoparia*, besom heath, is rarely grown in gardens; its dwarf form 'Minima' ('Pumila') is more often seen. Its value is in providing contrast between its dark glossy green leaves and dense habit of growth, and the coloured–leaved forms of other heathers. Its insignificant flowers are produced in April.

Erica *terminalis* (E. *stricta*), Corsican heath, is a native of the western Mediterranean, and is naturalised in Ireland. It is hardier than might be expected with such a home. Its habit is upright, up to 4 to 8 feet (1.2–2.4 m). The pale rose flowers last over a long period from June to October. It is distinct in its habit from all other tall-growing heaths and the old stems with their gnarled growth as seen in Bodnant Gardens have a peculiar charm of their own.

The Corsican heath Erica *terminalis*, flowering in the summer and autumn.

In the chalk garden so skilfully planted at Highdown near Worthing in Sussex by the late Sir Frederick Stern, I have seen seedlings growing from self-sown seeds on what is almost wholly chalky soil. I derive much pleasure from the attractive russet coloured dead flowers in the winter months, but find there is considerable repair work to be done to the branches after a snowfall.

Erica tetralix, cross–leaved heath, is native in northern and western Europe. It makes a small shrub up to 9 inches tall (22 cm). The dark green leaves are arranged in fours round the stem forming a cross. The rose coloured flowers are produced from June to October.

Erica vagans, Cornish heath, grows wild in south west Europe and Cornwall. It is a straggling shrub, forming a bush up to 2½ feet high (75 cm) and 4 feet across (1.2 m). The bell-shaped flowers are usually pale purplish pink with protruding stamens, produced from July to November.

HYBRIDS

There are five hybrids known between species of hardy *Erica*. None in the trade are the result of deliberate crosses and all are almost completely sterile.

E. × darleyensis (*E. herbacea × E. erigena*) was first noticed at the end of the last century at Darley Dale, Derbyshire. It is a neat shrub intermediate between its parents, and selections are listed on pp. 39 and 56.

E. × stuartii (praegeri) (*E. mackaiana × E. tetralix*). The parents are closely related and the hybrid is not easy to identify. It is quite common in Ireland, but unknown in Spain.

E. × watsonii (*E. ciliaris × E. tetralix*). This is intermediate between its parents, flowering from July onwards. It is to be found in Cornwall, Dorset and western France.

E. × williamsii (*E. tetralix × E. vagans*). Found ten times on the Lizard peninsula of Cornwall and nowhere else. It flowers from August onwards. All these four hybrids have the added

Above, *Erica × darleyensis*, one of the natural hybrids between hardy *Erica* species.
Below (left), 'Exeter', a selection of *Erica × veitchii*, which is a hybrid between the tree and Portuguese heaths, and (right) the dwarf *Daboecia × scotica*, another natural hybrid.

distinction that their young shoots are bright yellow, gold, pink or even red.

E. x veitchii (E. arborea x E.lusitanica). This has been noticed only three times and always in gardens, for the parents rarely grow near each other in the wild. Curiously, these three are somewhat more tender than their parents.

The only other hybrid among our heathers is *Daboecia x scotica (D. azorica x D. cantabrica).* This is larger than the first parent and smaller than the second and is hardier than both. It originated in Scottish gardens, hence its name (see also p. 48).

CULTIVARS

There are hundreds of cultivars from which to choose for the garden, and many are available from nurserymen. The main list below contains those which have been on trial at the R.H.S. Garden at Wisley and have had their value acknowledged by a First Class Certificate (F.C.C.) or Award of Merit (A.M.). A third accolade is the Award of Garden Merit (A.G.M.), also given by the R.H.S. to plants known to be of garden value throughout the British Isles.

The list is divided into three groups:
     A. Winter and spring flowering (p. 39)
     B. Summer flowering (p. 42)
     C. Foliage effect (p. 53).

The numbers in brackets after the cultivar name are measurements of height and, where possible, spread. The second figure, for spread, gives an indication of the plant spacing to use. These measurements were made from four–to–six–year–old plants in the trials and some further growth can be expected, although it will slow down with increasing age. However, plants left for many years can grow to a much greater size than is suggested from the figures below.

Winter and spring flowering

Erica × darleyensis (see p. 36)

Arthur Johnson. This is clearly distinguished by its long spikes of deep pink flowers up to 9 inches (23 cm) produced from November to May. (A.G.M.)

Darley Dale (2 ft; 60 cm) has been planted in large quantities and is one of the most attractive and reliable of all winter flowering heaths. It is very vigorous and will tolerate limey soil. It produces masses of pale pinkish mauve flowers from December to March. I know of no heath which will grow so well in difficult conditions. (A.M.)

Furzey (18 × 18 ins; 45 × 45 cm). Foliage very dark green, tinged and lightly tipped red. Flowers reddish purple, from February. (A.M.)

George Rendall (14 ins; 35 cm). A smaller 'Darley Dale' with deeper pinkish purple flowers from February. In spring and early summer the leaves are tinged creamy-pink at the tips. (A.G.M.)

J. W. Porter (1 × 2 feet; 30 × 60 cm). A rounded bush with red-purple flowers from February and dark green foliage. Spring foliage is bright cream and red.

Silberschmelze ('Molten Silver') (15 × 16 ins; 38 × 40 cm). This is also mistranslated as 'Silver Beads', 'Silver Bells', 'Silver Mist'. Winter foliage dark green. Flowers white, sometimes very slightly tipped pale pink, from January. (A.M.)

Erica erigena (E. mediterranea)

Irish Dusk (2 ft; 60 cm). Dark foliage and salmon pink flowers from October to May.

Golden Lady (12 ins; 30 cm). Golden yellow foliage throughout the year. White flowers in May. Slow growing.

Erica herbacea

Adrienne Duncan (9 × 10 in; 22 × 25 cm). A beautiful plant with very dark, bronze-green leaves and glowing crimson flowers. Rather similar to 'Vivellii', but a stronger plant. Flowers from late January to April.

Alan Coates (5 × 13 ins; 12 × 32 cm). Foliage dull bluish green. Flowers rose-purple, from mid-February. (A.M.)

Ann Sparkes (3½ × 14 ins; 9 × 35 cm). Foliage bright green at base changing to green tipped with yellow. Flowers reddish purple, from February. (A.M. for winter flowering and as a foliage plant.)

Cecilia M. Beale (6 × 9 ins; 15 × 22 cm). White flowers, January to March. Compact growth with erect flowering shoots.

December Red (7 × 17 ins; 18 × 42 cm). Foliage dark, dull slightly bluish green. Flowers cyclamen purple, from late November. (A.M.)

Eileen Porter (9 ins; 22 cm). Rich carmine-red flowers, October to April. A seedling from 'Praecox Rubra'. (A.M.)

Heathwood (6 × 14 ins; 15 × 35 cm). Deep pink flowers produced from January to April. Vigorous growth with dark bluish green foliage.

King George (6 × 12 ins; 15 × 30 cm). Compact growth, dark green foliage. Flowers deep rose pink, December to April. (A.G.M.)

Loughrigg (4 × 11 ins; 10 × 27 cm). Foliage dark bluish green. Flowers rosy purple, from early February. (A.M.)

March Seedling (6 × 20 ins; 15 × 50 cm). Purplish pink flowers February to April. Spreading habit.

Myretoun Ruby (6 × 18 ins: 15 × 45 cm). Dark green foliage, glowing ruby red flowers from February to April.

Pink Spangles (6 × 20 ins; 15 × 50 cm). Foliage dark green, lighter at tips. Flowers reddish purple, from January. (A.M.)

Pirbright Rose (8 × 16 ins; 20 × 40 cm). Foliage dull, dark bluish green tinged red here and there. Flowers reddish purple, from December. (A.M.)

Praecox Rubra (10 × 22 ins; 25 × 55 cm). Foliage dull medium to dark green. Flowers rosy red, from mid-January. (F.C.C.)

R. B. Cooke (6 × 18 ins; 15 × 45 cm). Mid-green foliage, and lavender coloured flowers, from December to May.

Above (left), Erica × darleyensis 'George Rendall' is smaller than the well-known 'Darley Dale', with deeper-coloured flowers (see p. 39).
(right) Erica erigena 'Irish Dusk', which flowers throughout winter and spring (see p. 39).
Below (left), two winter-flowering cultivars of Erica herbacea, 'Ann Sparkes' set off by 'Springwood White' (see pp. 41 and 42).
(right) The brilliant spring-flowering Erica herbacea 'Myretoun Ruby' (see p. 41).

Ruby Glow (6 × 20 ins; 15 × 50 cm). Foliage dull dark green. Flowers pale mauve ageing to reddish purple, from late January. (A.M.; A.G.M.)

Springwood Pink (6 × 13 ins; 15 × 32 cm). Foliage deep green. Flowers rose pink, from mid-January. (A.M.; A.G.M.)

Springwood White (6 × 18 ins; 15 × 45 cm). Foliage dark green. Flowers white, from early February. (F.C.C.; A.G.M.)

Sunshine Rambler (6 ins; 15 cm). A very good yellow foliage plant, which keeps its colour throughout the year. It has a spreading habit and the young shoots are golden yellow. Flowers pink to pale pink.

Vivellii (6 × 12 ins; 15 × 30 cm). Foliage dark green, changing to bronze in winter. Carmine–red flowers deepening at tips, from late January. (F.C.C.; A.G.M.)

Erica lusitanica

George Hunt (18 × 28 ins; 45 × 70 cm). Golden foliage in winter, slightly greener in summer. White flowers borne from March to April.

Superba (6 × ft; 1.8 m). Free flowering with bright purplish pink flowers from March to May. (A.M.; A.G.M.)

W. T. Rackliff (2 ft; 60 cm). The best white *lusitanica* cultivar. A compact hardy plant, with white flowers from February to May.

Summer flowering

Calluna vulgaris

Alba Jae (15 × 12 ins; 38 × 30 cm). Foliage bright medium green. Flowers white, from early August. (A.M.)

Alba Plena (12 × 12 ins; 30 × 30 cm). Foliage medium green. Double white flowers from mid-August. (A.M.; A.G.M.)

Alba Rigida (6 × 12 ins; 15 × 30 cm). Foliage bright medium green. Single white flowers from mid-July. (A.M.)

Alportii (24 × 18 ins; 60 × 45 cm). Foliage dark green. Flowers bright crimson-purple, August and September. (A.G.M.)

Annemarie (15 ins; 38 cm). A compact plant, with dark foliage and double flowers opening light pink and deepening to dark pink.

Applecross (2ft 6ins; 60 cm). A double pink-flowered cultivar with greyish foliage. Similar to 'H. E. Beale' (see p. 45), but the long flowering stems are taller. It keeps its foliage colour better during the winter than the 'H. E. Beale' group of cultivars. Flowers late August to October.

August Beauty (20 × 12 ins; 50 × 30 cm). Foliage fairly dark green. Flowers white, from end of July. (A.M.)

Aurea (12 × 10 ins; 30 × 25 cm). Foliage medium green to golden. Flowers single, purple, from end July. (A.M.)

Barnett Anley (18 × 12 ins; 45 × 30 cm). Foliage bright, fairly dark green. Single petunia-purple flowers in thick spikes, from mid-August. (F.C.C.; A.G.M.)

Beechwood Crimson (18 ins; 45 cm). Deep crimson flowers from August to September.

Beoley Gold (20 × 24 ins; 50 × 60 cm). Summer foliage light green, flushed gold and pale cream. Single white flowers from mid-August. (A.M. as a summer foliage and flowering plant.)

C. W. Nix (18 × 18 ins; 45 × 45 cm). Foliage dark dull green. Single magenta-rose flowers from early August. (A.M.)

Caerketton White (18 ins; 45 cm). Rather spreading habit. Foliage has light green tips. White flowers from June to July.

County Wicklow (12 × 12 ins; 30 × 30 cm). Foliage dark green. Double pink flowers, from late July. (F.C.C.; A.G.M.)

Cramond (15 × 36 ins; 38 × 90 cm). Foliage very dark green. Double flowers, reddish purple to purple fading almost to white on inner petals of some sprays, from early August. (A.M.)

Darkness (12 × 12 ins; 30 × 30 cm). Compact habit, dark green foliage, bright crimson flowers. August to September.

Drum-ra (12 × 12 ins; 30 × 30 cm). Foliage medium green. Flowers single white, from early August. (A.M.)

Elsie Purnell (20 × 20 ins; 50 × 50 cm). Foliage greyish green. Flowers double rose pink, from mid-August. (A.M.)

Fred J. Chapple (15 × 12 ins; 38 × 30 cm). Foliage for most of the year medium green, but in spring it has shades of green, gold, coral pink, and copper, and the tips are purplish red. Flowers single, purple, from mid-August. (A.M.)

Hammondii (30 ins; 75 cm). Dark green foliage and long spikes of single white flowers in August and September. Good for cutting. (A.G.M.)

H. E. Beale (24 ins; 60 cm). Foliage greyish green which tends to 'brown' in the winter, but recovers in the spring. Flowers double, silvery pink, from September to November. Good as a cut flower. (F.C.C., A.G.M.)

J. H. Hamilton (8 × 12 ins; 20 × 30 cm). Foliage dark green. Flowers from early August. Double, fuchsia-pink. (F.C.C., A.G.M.)

Joy Vanstone (14 × 28 ins; 35 × 70 cm). Foliage bright green at base of shoots, changing to lemon yellow on upper portions. Flowers single reddish purple, from mid-August. (A.M. as a summer foliage and flowering plant.)

Kinlochruel (12 × 9 ins; 30 × 22 cm). A double white-flowered sport from 'County Wicklow'. Flowering July/August. (F.C.C., A.M.).

Mair's Variety (24 ins; 60 cm). Foliage medium green. Flowers single, white, from late July. Very good for cutting as a 'white heather'. (F.C.C.)

Mullion (10 × 10 ins; 25 × 25 cm). Foliage medium green. Flowers single, orchid-purple, from mid-August. (A.M.)

My Dream (12 × 15 ins; 30 × 37 cm). A double white sport from 'H. E. Beale'. Upright growth. September to November.

Oxshott Common (30 × 30 ins; 75 × 75 cm). Foliage dull greyish green. Single purple flowers from mid-August. (A.M.)

Peter Sparkes (18 × 18 ins; 45 × 45 cm). A sport from 'H. E. Beale'. Flowers cyclamen purple, fading with age, from mid-August to October. (F.C.C., A.M., A.G.M.)

Pygmaea (5 × 8 ins; 12 × 20 cm). Foliage bright medium green. Flowers single, orchid-purple, from mid-August. (A.M.)

Radnor (10 × 18 ins; 25 × 45 cm). Foliage bright dark green. Flowers double reddish purple, flushed white at the base; from August. (A.M.)

Rosalind (10 × 14 ins; 25 × 35 cm). Foliage yellowish green. Single mallow-purple flowers, from late August. (A.M.)

Above (left), 'Beoley Gold' and (right) 'Cramond', two award-winning cultivars of *Calluna vulgaris* (see p. 43).
Below, *Calluna vulgaris* 'H. E. Beale', a good cut flower (see p. 45).

45

Serlei (36 × 24 ins; 90 × 60 cm). Foliage bright medium green. Single white flowers, from late August, continuing well into the autumn. (F.C.C.; A.G.M.)

Serlei Aurea (24 × 24 ins; 60 × 60 cm). Foliage bright greenish yellow. Single white flowers, from late August. (A.M.)

Silver Rose (16 ins; 40 cm). Silver grey foliage and single bright pink flowers from August.

Sir John Charrington (15 × 18 ins; 38 × 60 cm). Foliage golden-yellow, tinged scarlet and green on upper surfaces, under surfaces bright green. Single purple flowers from August. (A.M.)

Sister Anne (4 ins; 10 cm). Compact growth with silver-grey foliage, and pink flowers produced in August-September. (A.M. as foliage plant.)

Spring Cream (see p.55)

Spring Glow (see p.55)

Tib (10 × 12 ins; 25 × 32 cm). Foliage dark green. Double cyclamen purple flowers from late July. (F.C.C., A.M.)

Underwoodii (15 × 15 ins; 38 × 37 cm). Foliage medium to dark green. Clusters of single silver-pink to purple flower buds are produced, which do not open into flowers. They are effective from late August over a long period and undergo changes of colour as they age, remaining whitish at the base. A very unusual plant. (A.M.)

White Lion (2 ft; 60 cm). A completely prostrate form with emerald green foliage and white flowers borne on long horizontal racemes. The plants make a neat ground-hugging mat and are very suitable for a rock garden.

Daboecia

Alba is the name given to several white-flowered forms of *D. cantabrica* listed by nurserymen. The growth is similar to that of *D. cantabrica* but the foliage is paler and the flowers are larger.

Above (left), the summer-flowering *Calluna vulgaris* 'Silver Rose'. (right) *Calluna vulgaris* 'Tib' produces its double flowers from late summer.
Below, 'Praegerae', a delightful cultivar of *Daboecia cantabrica* (see p. 48).

Atropurpurea, another selected form of *D. cantabrica*, rich purple flowers. (A.G.M.)

Bicolor. This curious plant bears purple and white flowers and others are partly white and partly purple on the same stem. (A.G.M.)

David Moss (12 × 18 ins; 30 × 45 cm). Foliage dark glossy green. White flowers from June. (A.M.)

Praegerae (12 × 4 ins; 30 × 60 cm). Foliage bright medium green. Flowers deep pink to lighter salmon pink, from end of May. This is one of my favourites, but I have not found it so hardy as *D. cantabrica*. (A.M.)

Purpurea (18 × 23 ins; 45 × 57 cm). Foliage bright, medium dark green. Flower reddish purple at the base changing to purple towards the mouth, buds deep purple, from June. (A.M.)

Snowdrift (13 × 21 ins; 32 × 52 cm). Foliage bright green. White flowers from early June. (F.C.C.)

William Buchanan (*Daboecia × scotica*) (12 × 18 ins; 30 × 45 cm). Foliage dark glossy green. Flowers reddish purple, flowers from mid-June. (A.M.)

Erica ciliaris

Corfe Castle (12 × 12 ins; 30 × 30 cm). A compact grower with clear pink flowers. July to October.

David McClintock (15 × 12 ins; 37 × 30 cm). Light grey foliage, white flowers, deep pink tips. July/October. (A.M.)

Mrs C. H. Gill (12 ins; 30 cm). Foliage dark green, compact and bushy habit. Red flowers from July to October.

Stoborough (24 × 18 ins; 60 × 45 cm). Pearly white flowers, bright green foliage. July/October.

Erica cinerea

Alba Minor (7 × 14 ins; 17 × 34 cm). Foliage dark dull green. Single white flowers from early June. (F.C.C., A.M.)

Atrosanguinea Smith's Variety (8 × 20 ins; 20 × 50 cm). Foliage dark bluish green, young shoots bright green. Single reddish purple flowers from mid-June. (A.M.)

Cairn Valley (8 × 18 ins; 20 × 45 cm). Foliage dark green. Reddish purple flowers fading almost to white in places, from mid-June. (F.C.C., A.M.)

C. D. Eason (14 × 18 ins; 35 × 45 cm). Foliage very dark dull green. Bright rosy-red flowers from early June. (F.C.C., A.G.M.)

C. G. Best (12 ins; 30 cm). Long upright spikes of salmon-pink flowers produced from June to September.

Cevennes (12 × 14 ins; 30 × 35 cm). Foliage bright light green. Purple flowers from late June. (A.M.)

Cindy (12 ins; 30 cm). Bronze-green foliage, and purple flowers produced from July to September.

Duncan Fraser (10 × 22 ins; 25 × 55 cm). Summer foliage dark green with young tips light green. Flowers white, tinged pink, from mid-June. (A.M.)

Eden Valley (10 × 22 ins; 20 × 55 cm). Foliage dark fairly glossy green. Flowers white tipped phlox-purple from early June. (A.M., A.G.M.)

Fiddler's Gold (10 × 12 ins; 25 × 30 cm). Foliage light green, young shoots green flushed yellow and red. Flowers single, purple, from early June. (A.M.)

Glasnevin Red (10 × 19 ins; 25 × 47 cm). Foliage dark green. Flowers reddish purple, from early June. (A.M.)

Hookstone White (12 ins; 30 cm). Bright green foliage and long spikes of large white flowers.

Knap Hill Pink (10 × 14 ins; 25 × 35 cm). Foliage very dark dull green. Flowers rich pinkish purple, from early June. (F.C.C., A.M., A.G.M.)

Lavender Lady (8 × 23 ins; 20 × 58 cm). Foliage dark green. Flowers violet-purple, from mid-June. (A.M.)

P. S. Patrick (14 × 20 ins; 35 × 50 cm). Foliage dark glossy green, tips of shoots tinged dark purplish red. Flowers, bright reddish purple, from mid-June. (A.M., A.G.M.)

Pentreath (9 × 18 ins; 22 × 45 cm). Foliage dark green. Flowers rich purple, from mid-June. (A.M.)

Pink Foam (12 × 17 ins; 30 × 42 cm). Foliage dark green. Flowers whitish tinged mauve-pink, from mid-June. (A.M.)

Pink Ice (6 × 16 ins; 15 × 40 cm). Foliage bright, very dark green, tinted bronze in late winter and early spring. Flowers pink, from mid-June. (F.C.C., A.M.)

Plummer's Seedling (12 × 16 ins; 30 × 40 cm). Foliage dark green. Flowers rich reddish purple, from mid-June. (A.M.)

Rosea (9 × 26 ins; 22 × 65 cm). Foliage dark green. Flowers bright rose, from early June. (A.M., A.G.M.)

Stephen Davis (8 × 15 ins; 20 × 40 cm). Foliage dark green. Flowers reddish purple, from mid-June. (F.C.C.)

Tilford (12 × 23 ins; 30 × 57 cm). Foliage medium dark glossy green. Flowers purple, from mid-June. (A.M.)

Velvet Night (9 ins; 22 cm). One of the darkest-flowered cultivars available. Very deep purple flowers from June to August.

Vivienne Patricia (11 × 17 ins; 27 × 42 cm). Summer foliage very dark green with tips of shoots and stems of branchlets tinged dark red. Flowers purple, from mid-June. (A.M.)

Erica mackaiana

Dr Ronald Grey (6 ins; 15 cm). White flowers, borne from July to September.

Plena (6 ins; 15 cm). A low-growing plant with a spreading habit. Produces very attractive double rosy-white flowers in July and August.

Erica × stuartii (E. × praegeri)

Irish Lemon (12 ins; 25 cm). A compact plant, in which the new spring foliage is a bright clear lemon, which changes in summer to green. Erect habit and pale purple.

Erica tetralix

Alba Mollis (9 × 9 ins; 22 × 22 cm). White flowers, silvery-grey foliage turning green with age. July to September. (A.M.)

Con Underwood (9 × 9 ins; 22 × 22 cm). Large crimson flowers, grey–green foliage. June to October.

Pink Star (9 × 9 ins; 22 × 22 cm). Pink flowers, soft grey foliage. June to October.

Above (left), Erica cinerea 'Fiddler's Gold' and (right) 'Knap Hill Pink', both flowering from early June (see p. 49).
Below (left), 'Alba Mollis', a white-flowered cultivar of the cross-leaved heath Erica textralix.
(right) Erica vagans 'Mrs D. F. Maxwell', a beautiful cultivar of the Cornish heath (see p. 52).

Erica vagans

Cream (24 × 30 ins; 60 × 75 cm). Foliage dark dull green, young shoots brighter green. Flowers white, with bright red anthers when young changing to reddish brown, faint touch of pink at tips of buds, from late July. (A.M.)

Diana Hornibrook (15 × 12 ins; 38 × 30 cm). Foliage dark green, young foliage bright green. Flowers crimson, from end of July. (A.M.)

Holden Pink (18 × 19 ins; 45 × 47 cm). Foliage dark dull green. Flowers almost white flushed mallow–purple towards tips, from mid–July. (A.M.)

Kevernensis Alba (15 × 22 ins; 37 × 55 cm). Foliage dark green. Flowers white with bright brown stamens, from late July. (A.M.)

Lyonesse (18 ; 45 cm). The best white, with most attractive brown anthers. (A.G.M.)

Mrs D. F. Maxwell (12 × 20 ins; 30 × 50 cm). Foliage dark dull green with bright green tips. Flowers deep cerise with dark brown anthers, from early July. (F.C.C., A.G.M.) One of the finest heathers in cultivation.

St. Keverne (11 × 20 ins; 28 × 50 cm). Foliage dark green with brighter green tips. Flowers bright rose–cerise, tinged white towards the base, dark chocolate brown anthers, from mid–July. (F.C.C., A.G.M.)

Erica × watsonii

Cherry Turpin (12 ins; 30 cm). This hybrid resembles *E. ciliaris* more than its other parent *(E. tetralix)*, in having long racemes of pale pink flowers, rising from greyish green foliage. It has a long flowering period from July to the end of September.

Dawn (9 ins; 22 cm). Young foliage has orange-yellow tips. Rose-pink flowers produced from June to October.

Erica × williamsii

Gwavas (8 ins; 20 cm) is a good garden plant with golden yellow tips to the young leaves, and pale pink flowers from July to October.

P. D. Williams (18 ins; 45 cm). The young leaves are yellowish green, darkening with age. Pink bell-shaped flowers are borne from July to October.

For foliage effect

Several plants are valued for their coloured foliage, and a number have received awards as foliage plants.

Calluna vulgaris

Anthony Davis (15 × 18 ins; 38 × 45 cm). Grey-green foliage, and white flowers are borne in August-September.

Beoley Gold (see p. 43)

Carole Chapman (15 × 15 ins; 38 × 38 cm). Foliage light green at base of shoots, pale yellow or golden yellow on upper portion of shoots, green on undersides. Single white flowers from end of July. (A.M. summer foliage)

Gold Haze (18 × 10 ins; 45 × 25 cm). Foliage bright golden yellow. Single white flowers from early August. (F.C.C., A.G.M.)

Golden Carpet (5 × 24 ins; 12 × 60 cm). Foliage cream, tipped golden yellow, upper surface green, stems dull red. Flowers reddish purple, from early August. (A.M. summer foliage).

Golden Feather (15 × 24 ins; 38 × 60 cm). Foliage golden-yellow, with light green showing through and tipped dark red. Single mauve flowers from late August. (F.C.C. summer and winter foliage).

Hirsuta Typica (18 × 24 ins; 45 × 60 cm). Foliage greyish green, sometimes giving the impression of silver. Single purple flowers from mid-August. (F.C.C. as a grey foliage plant: A.G.M.)

Humpty Dumpty (6 × 9 ins; 15 × 22 cm). Hummock-like growth, resembling some dwarf conifers. White flowers borne in August - September. Rather shy flowering.

Joy Vanstone. See p. 45.

Multicolour (6 × 12 ins; 15 × 30 cm). Foliage yellowish green, tipped golden and coral, but readily reverts to green. Single purple flowers, from late July. (A.M. as a plant for winter effect and for summer flower).

Oxshott Common. See p. 45.

Rannoch (12 × 17 ins; 30 × 42 cm). Foliage light green on basal growths, upper part of shoots golden flushed bright red, light green on undersides. Stems on young shoots deep pink. Single purple flowers are produced from late July. (A.M. as a summer foliage plant.)

Robert Chapman (10 × 14 ins; 25 × 35 cm). Foliage in winter medium green overlaid orange-red to scarlet-red. Single rose purple flowers from mid-August. (A.M. as a plant for winter effect: A.G.M.)

Rosalind. See p. 45.

Serlei Aurea. See p. 46.

Silver Queen (6 × 9 ins: 15 × 22 cm). Silver-grey foliage, and mauve flowers produced in August-September.

Sir John Charrington. See p. 46.

Sister Anne. See p. 46.

Spring Cream (18 ins; 45 cm). Cream tipped foliage in spring, white flowers produced in August-September.

Spring Glow (18 ins; 45 cm). The chief value of this cultivar is the colour of the young spring growth – a rich mixture of golden yellow and deep flame-coloured orange, rising from dark green shoots. It is a strong-growing plant with thick foliage. The flowers, in August and September, are an attractive mauve.

Sunset (15 × 26 ins; 37 × 65 cm). Undersides of shoots light bright green tipped yellow, upper sides tipped and tinged red, also tinged creamy yellow and orange. Produces a few pink flowers in August and September. (F.C.C. as a winter foliage plant.)

Erica ciliaris

Aurea (9 ins; 22 cm). Golden yellow foliage, with pink flowers in July-August. Not a robust grower.

Erica cinerea

Fiddler's Gold. See p. 49.

Golden Drop (6 × 9 ins; 15 × 22 cm). Copper coloured foliage in summer turning to reddish in winter. Pink flowers produced from June to August.

Above (left), *Calluna vulgaris* 'Gold Haze' and (right) 'Golden Feather', two heathers with excellent foliage effect (see p. 53).
Below (left), the striking winter foliage of *Calluna vulgaris* 'Robert Chapman'.
(right) *Erica herbacea* 'Foxhollow', valuable for its summer and winter foliage (see p. 56).

Golden Hue (12 ins; 30 cm). Golden summer foliage changing to red as winter approaches. Pink flowers produced from June to August.

Windlebrooke (8 × 10 ins; 20 × 25 cm). Light golden–yellow foliage in summer turning to orange red in winter. Purple flowers. July to September.

E. × darleyensis

Jack H. Brummage (10 × 12 ins; 25 × 30 cm). Foliage bright light green, young shoots golden yellow, green at tips with bright red stems. Reddish purple flowers with dark chocolate brown stamens from mid–November. (A.M. for summer foliage).

Erica erigenea

Golden Lady. See p. 39.

Erica herbacea

Ann Sparkes. See p. 41.

Aurea (8 × 24 ins; 20 × 60 cm). Foliage bright green and lemon yellow, some shoots flushed pink at the tips. Deep pink flowers from January to April. (A.M. for summer foliage.)

Foxhollow (9 ins; 22 cm). Foliage golden yellow in summer, turning to deep gold, flecked red, in winter. Pale pink flowers.

Sunshine Rambler. See p. 42.

Erica vagans

Valerie Proudley (6 × 13 ins; 15 × 32 cm). Foliage bright lemon yellow throughout the year. A few white flowers from early September. (A.M. for summer and winter foliage).

Shrubs to use in the heather garden

In most established heather gardens, very effective use can be made of either single specimen shrubs which have been carefully sited, or groups of a kind which either blend or contrast with the planting scheme. The choice is wide and the selection need not be restricted to the Erica family.

I have seen very good use made of the following:

Acer palmatum 'Dissectum' and 'Dissectum Atropurpureum'. These are dense growing Japanese maples which form rounded, slow growing bushes with fine divided leaves, particularly beautiful in spring and autumn. To be planted as single specimens.

Andromeda polifolia, bog rosemary. A dwarf shrub of the Erica family with narrow glaucous leaves having a white under-surface. The soft pink, pitcher-shaped flowers are borne in terminal racemes in May.

Arctostaphylos uva–ursi, bearberry. A trailing evergreen with white to pink clusters of pitcher–shaped flowers in June.

Berberis. There are a few small–growing berberis, both deciduous and evergreen, which are effective. Among these are *B. thunbergii* 'Atropurpurea Nana' and *B. wilsoniae*, both of which are deciduous; and *B. candidula*, *B.* × *stenophylla* 'Coccinea' and 'Corallina Compacta' and *B. verruculosa*, all of which are evergreen.

Bruckenthalia spiculifolia, Balkan heather. A dwarf heath–like evergreen with terminal racemes of rose–pink bell–shaped flowers from June.

Cytisus. Three useful brooms are *C.* × *beanii*, dwarf with yellow flowers; *C.* × *praecox*, creamy flowers in May, and *C.* 'Allgold', with rich yellow flowers also in May.

× *Gaulnettya wisleyensis* 'Wisley Pearl'. A small evergreen shrub which is a hybrid between *Gaultheria shallon* and *Pernettya mucronata*. It is of value in autumn and winter when it bears heavy crops of large ox–blood red fruits.

Gaultheria. *G. hispida* is a low growing evergreen with white flowers followed by most attractive white fruits. *G. miqueliana* has white flowers followed by white or pink fruits. *G. procumbens*

is an evergreen carpeter, particularly attractive in autumn and winter when it bears bright red fruits.

Kalmia angustifolia. An evergreen shrub which tends to spread by underground stems. Rosy red flowers in June.

Ledum groenlandicum (Labrador tea). A very hardy evergreen with terminal clusters of white flowers from April to June.

Leiophyllum buxifolium. A neat growing evergreen shrub about 12 inches high (30 cm), with lovely pink flower buds*which open to white in May and June. This makes a most attractive 'drift' in a heather garden and is one of my favourites.

Leucothoe fontanesiana 'Nana'. This is the dwarf from of the species and is a real asset to give foliage contrast among heathers. Its leathery green leaves take on bronze–purple tints in autumn and winter. The white flowers are borne in pendent racemes in spring.

Menziesia ciliicalyx. A small deciduous shrub of the Erica family which always attracts attention, both for its hairy leaves and cream to soft purple flowers in May. The variety *purpurea* has rose-purple flowers.

Pernettya mucronata is a vigorous evergreen with dark leaves with spiny tips. In May and June the white heath-like flowers are borne in great profusion, but as male and female flowers are borne on different plants it is necessary to include male plants in the groups to ensure good crops of berries. Nurserymen usually keep stocks of these separated from the fruiting forms. There are numerous named cultivars; 'White Pearl' and 'Bell's Seedling' are two of the best.

Rhododendron. I feel that if any rhododendrons are included they should not detract from the heathers, for there could be a tendency to be looking at rhododendrons with heathers among them, rather than the reverse. The rhododendron that I would plant first and foremost is the the dwarf form of *Rhododendron racemosum*, 'Forrest's Dwarf', still propagated under Forrest's collecting number 19404, which grows to about 2 feet (60 cm); the flowers are bright pink, borne in clusters along the shoots. 'Fittra' (mallow purple flowers) and 'Spinulosum' (apricot pink) are two hybrids of *R. racemosum* that also suit the heather garden.

Above, *Acer palmatum* 'Dissectum' and, below (left), *Gaultheria procumbens* are two shrubs which associate particularly well with heathers (see p. 57).
(right) The dwarf *Rhododendron ferrugineum*, a European native (see p.60).

Other rhododendrons I would choose are R. *ferrugineum* – up to 4 feet (1.2m), tubular rosy crimson flowers; R. *hirsutum* – up to 4 feet (1.2 m), with rose-pink to scarlet flowers and its hybrid 'Myrtifolium' lilac pink flowers; R. *lepidostylum* – up to 3 feet (90 cm), bluish green leaves, pale yellow flowers; R. *micranthum* – up to 3 feet (90 cm), flowers milky white; R. *pubescens* – up to 4 feet (1.2 m), flowers rose to pinkish white; R. *tephropeplum* – up to 6 feet (1.8 m), flowers pink to purplish; R. *trichostomum* – up to 4 feet (1.2 m), flowers rose or white.

Sorbus reducta. A dwarf mountain ash, forming a suckering shrub from 2 to 3 feet high (60–90 cm). The leaves turn to bronze and reddish purple in the autumn, the fruits are white flushed rose. This looks very much at home as a 'clump' among heathers.

Ulex gallii. A dwarf gorse, flowering in summer and autumn. This in the smaller scale of a garden gives the effect of the common gorse in the wild setting of the moorland. Another dwarf gorse which is at its best in September, is *U. minor.* Both species are best planted in dry hungry soil conditions and I find them particularly good among *Erica cinerea* and its cultivars.

Vaccinium myrtillus. A native whortleberry and blueberry seen in quantities on our moorlands, where it forms masses of suckering angular shoots. The greenish pink flowers from April to June are followed by dark purple edible berries. This is worth growing among heathers for the effect of its slender branches alone, and I like it particularly in the winter after the leaves have fallen.

Vaccinium vitis-idaea, cowberry. Another British native plant, a dwarf creeping evergreen, with small shiny leaves and white to pink terminal racemes of bell-shaped flowers from June to August. The edible red fruits taste acid.

CONIFERS

I like to include a selection of dwarf and slow growing conifers among heathers. It is difficult to make a choice from the wealth of material available, but the following list is a selection which should suit most tastes. At the same time I am fully conscious that many others have been omitted and I hope this fact will create the urge to visit specialist nurserymen to see the very wide range which is grown.

Upright, including conical and pyramidal forms

Chamaecyparis lawsoniana, Lawson's cypress. 'Ellwoodii' with feathery grey-green foliage, and 'Ellwood's Gold' with yellow-tinged tips to the branches. 'Minima Aurea' is conical in outline with golden yellow foliage.

Chamaecyparis obtusa. 'Nana Gracilis' is cone-shaped with dark green foliage.'Tetragona Aurea' has golden yellow foliage, and may in time grow to a small tree.

Chamaecyparis pisifera, Sawara cypress. 'Boulevard' has a conical habit, steely blue foliage, tinted purple in winter.

Chamaecyparis thyoides, white cypress. 'Andelyensis' is rather columnar in habit with dark bluish green foliage. 'Ericoides' is cone-shaped with green foliage in summer changing to bronze or plum coloured in winter.

Juniperus virginiana, pencil cedar. 'Sky Rocket' has very narrow columnar growth and blue-grey foliage.

Picea glauca. 'Albertiana Conica' is cone shaped, with dense growth with bright green foliage.

Thuja occidentalis, white cedar. 'Rheingold' is conical in habit, the rich deep foliage shaded amber, particularly effective in winter, but grows to 8 feet (2.4 m).

Thuja orientalis 'Elegantissima' is columnar in habit. Golden-yellow foliage tinged old-gold, changing to green in the winter.

Thuja plicata, western red cedar. 'Rogersii' has a conical habit, gold and bronze-coloured foliage.

Rounded or flat topped including forms which tend to spread

Abies balsamea, balsam fir. 'Hudsonia' is flat topped, with dark green foliage.

Chamaecyparis lawsoniana 'Pygmaea Argentea' of rounded habit, and dark bluish green foliage with silvery-white tips.

Cryptomeria japonica, Japanese cedar. 'Bandai-sugi' makes a compact bush which tends to become rugged with age. It has green foliage. 'Jindai-sugi' is more upright in growth, tending to spread out into a flat top, but with an attractive irregular branching habit.

Picea abies, Norway spruce. 'Gregoryana' of rounded habit, and sea green foliage; a very popular dwarf conifer.

Picea mariana, black spruce. 'Nana' has a globular habit with grey-green foliage.

Picea pungens 'Compacta' is a flat-topped blue spruce.

Pinus mugo, mountain pine, is a strong growing large shrub or small tree which is more suitable for the larger heather garden, but there are dwarf forms available.

Pinus sylvestris, Scots pine. 'Beuvronensis' is a dwarf with grey or bluish green foliage.

Thuja orientalis. 'Aurea Nana' has a globular habit with light yellow green foliage. 'Hillieri' makes a compact medium–sized bush with soft yellow green foliage changing to green in winter.

Thuja plicata 'Hillieri' is rounded in habit, with moss–like green foliage.

Thujopis dolobrata 'Nana', a spreading flat-topped form with bright green foliage, tending to take on bronze tints in winter.

Ground cover

Junipers are well suited as a ground cover to provide contrast among the heather foliage.

Juniperus communis, common juniper. 'Repanda' is a dwarf spreading juniper with green foliage tending to become slightly bronze in winter.

Juniperus conferta is prostrate growing with bright apple green foliage and a white band on the upper surface.

Juniperus sabina, savin. 'Tamariscifolia' is an old favourite, growing into a dense flat topped spreading bush with bright green foliage.

Above, *Vaccinium vitis-idaea* growing with heathers (see p. 60).
Below (left), a group of conifers of various shapes, with *Juniperus conferta* in front.
(right) *Juniperus sabina* 'Tamariscifolia' against a background of *Daboecia*.

Books

Heathers in Colour by B. and V. Proudley. 192pp. 1974. Blandford Press.
Heathers by Adrian Bloom. 32 pp. 1972. Jarrolds, Norwich.
The Heather Garden by Harry van der Laar. 160pp. 1978. Collins.
Heaths and Heathers by T. L. Underhill. 256pp. 1972. David & Charles.
Pocket Guide to Heather Gardening by G. Yates. 4th Edition 1978.

Two other good books now out–of–print are:
The English Heather Garden by D. Fife Maxwell and P. S. Patrick, 184pp. 1966. Macdonald, London.
The Heather Garden by Fred J. Chapple, 190pp. Revised 1964. Collingridge, London.

I have had much valuable help in the preparation of this booklet from members of the staff at Wisley, in particular from Miss A. V. Brooks on diseases, from Mr A. Halstead on pests and from Mr R. Waite on propagation.

THE HEATHER SOCIETY

This Society was founded to foster interest in the growing of hardy heaths and heathers. Its members receive a bulletin three times a year and a year book, and meetings and garden visits are also arranged. For further details write to: Mrs A. Small, Denbeigh, All Saints Road, Creeting St Mary, Ipswich, Suffolk.